THE GOD-FIRST LIFE

UNCOMPLICATE YOUR LIFE, **GOD'S WAY**

STOVALL WEEMS
WITH KEVIN AND SHERRY HARNEY

ZONDERVAN®

ZONDERVAN

The God-First Life Study Guide
Copyright © 2014 by Stovall Weems

This title is also available as a Zondervan ebook. Visit www.zondervan.com/ebooks.

Requests for information should be addressed to:

Zondervan, 3900 *Sparks Dr. SE, Grand Rapids, Michigan* 49546

ISBN 978-0-310-69799-2

Published in association with the literary agency of Fedd & Company, Inc., Post Office Box 341973, Austin, Texas 78734

Cover design: Studio Gearbox
Interior design: Matthew Van Zomeren

First Printing June 2014 / Printed in the United States of America

CONTENTS

A WORD FROM STOVALL WEEMS

When I was growing up, I occasionally went to church, but God wasn't really a big part of my life. I would say I was definitely Christian in my beliefs, but as a young person, my focus was on doing what a lot of young people do—partying and having a good time. I believed God existed, but I didn't think there was much more to faith in God than that.

About midway through college, something changed. I had an aunt who was praying for me, and God was really drawing me to him. I found myself tiring of the typical college party lifestyle. The things I was involved in began to feel very shallow and temporary. Partying, studying, working, partying—I knew there had to be more than this, and I began actively seeking.

I was at a secular university, but I chose to major in religious studies. If Jesus was the truth, I wanted to know. I personally believe that's what goes on in every human being. We come to a point where we long for more. By God's grace, in my seeking I found Jesus and right there in the middle of the college party scene, I surrendered my life to him.

I found the experience, presence, and forgiveness of Jesus amazing. I wanted to follow him with everything I had and was. But it wasn't easy. At the time I invited Christ into my life, I was part of the roughest fraternity on campus and worked in a bar.

Not recommended.

It was a confusing place and time. As I moved forward in my new-found faith, I faced tougher questions, harder choices, and stronger temptations than I knew what to do with.

I was reading the Bible, and sometimes it spoke directly to me and provided exactly the answer I needed. But other times the Bible seemed totally unrelated to the things I was dealing with. For every one thing I understood about God or the world, there were about ten others that seemed confusing, even unfair.

One day I was walking to class, considering all the questions racing through my head, and God brought to mind something I'd read in the Bible: "Seek first his kingdom and his righteousness, and all these things will be given to you as well" (Matthew 6:33). This was the turning point. God spoke powerfully to me in that moment. *Seek me above all else*, he said. *Put me first.*

If I would truly put God first—regardless of how I felt or whether I completely understood it—then he would take care of *"all these things."* I didn't do it perfectly. I didn't have it all figured out. But this one small verse from the mouth of Jesus changed everything for me. My faith started moving from my head down deep into my heart. From then on, Matthew 6:33 became my compass. It seemed so simple, so tangible. There were a lot of things I couldn't do—or didn't even know to do. But I could do that. I could do my best to put God first.

This simple idea has changed my life and the lives of countless Christians through the ages. I want to invite you on a journey of discovery where you will learn to live a God-first life. Over the coming six weeks you will learn, pray, laugh, struggle, and rejoice with your group members. I am confident that if you are willing to invest yourself in this experience, you will find new order, direction, strength, and joy in every part of your life as you learn to live the God-first life.

OF NOTE

The quotations interspersed throughout this study guide and the intro-
ductory comments are excerpts from the book *The God-First Life* and
the video curriculum of the same name by Stovall Weems. All other
resources, including the small group questions, introductions, and
between-sessions materials, have been written by Kevin and Sherry
Harney in collaboration with Stovall Weems.

YOUR LIFE, GOD'S WAY

An Invitation to Seek God's Kingdom First

Some passages in the Bible seem complex and deep the
first time you read them. Other passages feel clear and
transparent right away. Then, there are passages that
seem to make sense, but with time, they drive you deeper
and deeper into the heart and presence of God. One such
passage comes from the lips of Jesus. If you read it, if you
really get it, and if you let this passage get ahold of you, it
could turn your whole life upside down!
Here it is:

But seek first his kingdom and his righteousness,
and all these things will be given to you as well.

(Matthew 6:33)

INTRODUCTION

Have you ever "Yelped" something?

If you have a smart phone, you might have an app called Yelp. If you do, you can be traveling almost anywhere and find a great restaurant quickly and easily. You just touch the icon for your Yelp app and type in the kind of food you want. For instance, type "Mexican food," press the search button, and in a matter of moments you will have a list of Mexican restaurants right there on your phone. You can arrange them by popularity, distance from your location, or price range; you can even pull up customer reviews and pictures of the food and restaurant. Amazing!

Have you ever read the Bible on your phone or a tablet? It is easy if you have the Bible Gateway app. This little tool supplies reading plans, allows you to listen to the Bible, provides a place for you to take and keep notes on what you are learning, and much more — all of this in the palm of your hand. Powerful!

There are apps that tell you the weather in any part of the world, others that help you lose weight as they monitor your eating and exercise. There are apps that entertain you with games, provide free music of any genre you like, allow you to follow your favorite sport or team, and the list goes on and on. More and more apps are marketed with each passing day and most of them are free or very inexpensive. They are also, for the most part, quite easy to use. A few touches of your finger, ask a question or two, and the world unfolds before you.

But apps are simple for us because under the surface of the recognizable icon on our phone and the user-friendly app is an incredibly complex serving system. Someone invented it, coded it, designed it, and maintains it. What seems intuitive and straightforward to us is actually quite sophisticated. If you could look behind the scenes, you would be amazed at all that is going on so that you can find your Mexican restaurant, check out the weather for next Wednesday in Sydney, Australia, or look up Matthew 6:33 on your phone.

Sometimes, when something appears to be simple and straightforward, it is actually deeper and more complex than we realize at first glance. Some Bible verses are like this. One of the greatest examples of this is a simple statement that comes directly from the mouth and heart of Jesus: "But seek first his kingdom and his righteousness, and all these things will be given to you as well" (Matthew 6:33). Seems simple, doesn't it? The idea is actually very easy to understand. But living out this truth will take a lifetime!

> Putting things into their proper order
> leads to a balanced, blessed life.

TALK ABOUT IT

If you are familiar with apps, what is a favorite app you have on your phone or tablet and why is it helpful to you? How does this app take something complex and make it simple?

or

Tell about when you first began to experience a drawing toward God and a desire to understand that he has a plan for your life.

> God's way is better than ours.

VIDEO TEACHING NOTES

As you watch the video teaching segment for session 1, featuring Stovall Weems, use the following outline to record anything that stands out to you.

One man's journey toward the God-first life

Matthew 6:33: Seek God first and everything you need will be added

The God–First app is Matthew 6:33

Blessings of a new family, new life, new freedom

The world's recipe for a happy life

The answer to the happy life is putting God first

When order is restored, blessing is released

Holiness leads to happiness

> Whatever has first place in your life
> directs how you live it.

VIDEO DISCUSSION AND BIBLE STUDY

1. Stovall tells about becoming a follower of Jesus as a college student, while working at a bar. When did you become a Christian (or maybe you are still investigating) and how has God changed your life since that time?

2. Even after we become Christians, we can still have questions about God, Jesus, the Bible, heaven, among other things. What was a question you grappled with after becoming a Christian that eventually made sense?

   Why is it okay to love Jesus and follow him and still have questions?

3. **Read:** Matthew 6:33. How can seeking first God's kingdom, his will, and his righteousness help make sense of the questions we might struggle with?

4. In the times and seasons of life when we actually seek first God's kingdom and his will for our lives, things often seem to fall into place and make sense. Tell about a time or a season in your life when you really devoted your heart and life to seeking God's will. How did God come alive, show up, and work during this time?

> God never intended us to live a complex or complicated life.

5. In Matthew 6:33, Jesus teaches us that order is critical. Seek *first* his kingdom. What have you noticed happens in your life when you seek God's kingdom first?

What happens when you seek *your* will, *your* desires, and *your* ways first?

6. When you became a Christian, you were ushered into a new family. Tell how God impacted your life through your new brothers and sisters after you followed Jesus and became part of his church.

7. **Read:** Proverbs 3:5–6. How do these wise words of Proverbs echo the heartbeat of Matthew 6:33?

How does trusting the Lord with all our heart help us seek him first?

8. Stovall makes this provocative statement: "When order is restored, blessing is released!" Respond to this. Do you agree? If so, why? Do you disagree? If so, why?

9. **Read:** 1 Peter 1:13–16. How can walking and living in holiness increase our happiness?

How can turning from God's ways and living with self-centered desires (rather than a God-first life orientation) rob us of joy and happiness?

> When we have the proper order in our life, happiness is a by-product.

10. How have you experienced the blessing and happiness of God as a direct result of setting God-honoring priorities and seeking him first in your life?

What is one new priority you might begin today, and how can your group members pray as you take this next step into the God-first life?

> Jesus wasn't against happiness—
> he just redefined how to get it.

CLOSING PRAYER

Take time as a group to pray in any of the following directions:

- Thank God for people that he placed in your life who prayed for you, reached out to you, and showed you what a God-first life could look like.
- Thank God for drawing you to himself and for showing you his love and grace.
- Ask the Holy Spirit to help you see when you are being drawn toward living in a way that puts yourself or other people first, rather than God.
- Pray for God to help you find happiness in seeking him first.
- Thank Jesus for showing you what a God-first life looks like and pray that you will be more like him.

> The God-first life is predicated on order.

BETWEEN SESSIONS

PERSONAL REFLECTION

Take time in personal reflection to think about the following questions. If you would like, use the journaling space at the end of this session to record your thoughts.

- What are some of the questions you still have about faith and the Bible? How can you seek God first even as you grapple with these questions?
- In what areas of your life do you tend to put yourself or your will first? How can you be proactive and decide in advance how you want to respond in a God-first way the next time you face this temptation?
- Who can you pray for and encourage to live a God-first life? How might God use you to bless them like he used other people to direct you toward a life that seeks him first?

> God-first living is the only way to receive the blessing we instinctively seek.

PERSONAL ACTIONS

GET IT IN YOUR HEART AND MIND

Take time this week to commit Matthew 6:33 to memory. Then begin each day repeating the verse a few times, reflecting deeply on its simple invitation and asking God to help you to live in its truth throughout your day. Again, at the end of the day, when you lie down for the night, repeat the verse a few more times. Ask God to help you see where you can seek him first tomorrow.

LOOKING BACK AND REMEMBERING

Reflect back on times in your journey of faith when you really sought God first and pursued his will with passion and consistency. Make a list of five good things that happened in your life during this season of seeking God first:

1.

2.

3.

4.

5.

In moments when you are tempted to seek your own will or lean on your own understanding rather than trust in God, look at this list and reflect on the happiness and blessing that comes when you are living a God–first life.

> When order is restored, blessing is released.

LOOKING FORWARD AND PREPARING TO LIVE A GOD-FIRST LIFE

Consider three areas of your life where you can be tempted to make decisions or take actions that are *not* putting God first. These could be areas you have put yourself first in the past or tended to lean on your own understanding.

Area #1: Area of life I can be tempted to put myself first and seek my own wisdom rather than putting God first:

List some of the consequences and costs you have faced by not living a God-first life in this specific area of your life:

-
-
-
-

Write down what a God-first response would look like the next time you face this area of potential temptation.

Pray for strength and wisdom to respond in a way that clearly puts God first the next time you are in this situation.

Area #2: Area of life I can be tempted to put myself first and seek my own wisdom rather than putting God first:

List some of the consequences and costs you have faced by not living a God-first life in this specific area of your life:

-
-
-
-

Write down what a God-first response would look like the next time you face this area of potential temptation.

Pray for strength and wisdom to respond in a way that clearly puts God first the next time you are in this situation.

Area #3: Area of life I can be tempted to put myself first and seek my own wisdom rather than putting God first:

List some of the consequences and costs you have faced by not living a God-first life in this specific area of your life:

-

-

-

-

Write down what a God-first response would look like the next time you face this area of potential temptation.

Pray for strength and wisdom to respond in a way that clearly puts God first the next time you are in this situation.

> We yield to a God whose authority brings
> an empowering blessing,
> not an oppressive burden.

RECOMMENDED READING

As you reflect on what God is teaching you through this session, read chapters 1–2 of *The God-First Life* by Stovall Weems. In preparation for the next session, read chapter 3.

JOURNAL, REFLECTIONS, AND NOTES

_____

_____

_____

_____

_____

_____

_____

_____

_____

_____

_____

_____

_____

_____

_____

_____

_____

_____

_____

_____

_____

_____

_____

ADOPTED INTO GOD'S FAMILY

Understand Your Position as a Member of God's Family

We all have a family. Some are healthy, close, strong, and we look back on our upbringing with fond memories. Others are unhealthy, fragmented, dysfunctional, and we can spend years trying to heal from the pain of our past. No matter how good or tough our upbringing, we are adopted into a new family when we come to God through faith in Jesus. When we receive the grace of our heavenly Father offered through his Son Jesus, we become part of God's forever family. When we accept this and embrace it as a gift, we discover joy, blessing, and meaning that can be found in no other place.

INTRODUCTION

Status is a precarious thing. We can work for years to reach a certain point in life and then discover—in a flash!—that the position is gone. Interestingly, many of the words that describe the painful process of losing status begin with the letter "D":

- *Disbarment.* A person who has studied for years, earned a law degree, passed the state bar exam, and served the community well can lose her license to practice law. By behaving in an unethical manner, breaking the law, or willfully disregarding the interests of her client, she can be disbarred and have her whole life turned upside down.
- *Defrocking.* A licensed minister or priest can receive a seminary degree, work for the church, and invest his life in serving others. Then, if he crosses ethical, financial, or moral boundaries, he can have his ordination and ministry taken away.
- *Demotion.* A business leader can show up at work one day feeling secure and in charge. But, if the company is struggling, if stocks are plummeting, if she makes a mistake in judgment or behavior, a demotion could change the way everyone sees her ... and also the way she sees herself.
- *Dishonorable discharge.* In the military, one of the worst things a person can face is being dismissed without honor. One day he has rank and authority, wears a uniform, and is respected. The next day all of it can be taken away.

In a world of temporary honor, influence, and authority, is there anything that is absolutely secure? In a life that feels like a roller coaster filled with unexpected ups and downs, what can we hold onto with confidence? God gives a hope-filled answer to both of these questions. When we place our faith in Jesus Christ, we are called "sons of God" and "daughters of God." We are adopted into God's family forever, a status no one can strip away or remove. Nor can we behave so badly that God will stop calling us his beloved children. In an uncertain world where people are disbarred, defrocked, demoted, dishonorably discharged, downgraded, dismissed, and disqualified, this is wonderful news!

> When we come into God's kingdom,
> we come into his family.

TALK ABOUT IT

Tell one thing about your family system or history that is unique (in a good, fun, or interesting way).

or

What is a characteristic or trait in your family that seems to run through more than one generation?

> God has not called us to do life alone.

VIDEO TEACHING NOTES

As you watch the video teaching segment for session 2, featuring Stovall Weems, use the following outline to record anything that stands out to you.

The kingdom of God is the rule and reign of Jesus

No matter what you do, you are always part of your family; when you have faith in Jesus, you are part of God's family forever

Every Christian has both a position and a function in God's family

Every family has a history

Our position in Christ is secure

The first step of learning our function is getting planted in a local church

Our position gives us access, but our function gives us impact

God's design and blueprint

VIDEO DISCUSSION AND BIBLE STUDY

1. How have you experienced God's love, care, or provision as your heavenly Father?

> To fully experience the God-first life, you
> absolutely must come to understand
> God's unmistakable love for you and
> complete acceptance of you.

2. What is one joy you have experienced as you have become part of God's family and discovered you have brothers and sisters in faith?

   What is one challenge you have faced coming into the church—the family of God—and how are you seeking to overcome this challenge?

3. **Read:** Hebrews 10:23–25. When we discover the importance and power of being part of God's family, we take being part of the church very seriously. What does this passage teach us about the value and significance of our connection with our brothers and sisters in Christ?

> The local church is the soil necessary
> for your life to flourish.

4. How are you strengthened in faith when you do *one* of the following:

❑ Hold to the hope found in Jesus Christ alone

❑ Spur on brothers and sisters in Christ to live in love and extend good deeds to others

❑ Receive exhortation from other believers to walk with Jesus and love others

❑ Regularly attend church services and growth opportunities in your local church

❑ Encourage other believers and receive encouragement from them

5. Stovall talks about the fact that we have both a position and a function in God's family. What is the difference between these two ideas? Why is this an important distinction?

6. Stovall says that the first step to discovering your function in God's family is becoming a part of a healthy local church. How have you discovered your function and purpose through being part of a local congregation, and how has finding a place to serve helped in this process?

> Each of us has a unique purpose
> and function in the family of God.

7. **Read:** Psalm 92:12–15 and Psalm 1:3. What do our lives look like when we are planted in the rich soil of a local church and our roots are growing deep?

8. What are some of the temptations that cause us to wander and not send down deep roots in a local church?

How can we battle these temptations?

9. Describe how you are planted in the local church today (or were some time in the past) and how God is using you to be a blessing to others. What is it like to experience God working through you?

10. How can staying rooted in a local church help us grow in maturity? What is one way you can get more rooted and connected in your church in the coming month?

> Position gives us access, but
> function gives us impact.

CLOSING PRAYER

Take time as a group to pray in any of the following directions:

- Thank God for your family of origin and praise him for the good things passed on to you by your family.
- Lift up praise to God for the church you are part of and pray for your church leaders as they seek to serve faithfully.
- Thank God that there is nothing that could remove his love from you and nothing that could take you out of his forever family.
- Pray for people in your church family who might be feeling marginalized or forgotten.
- Ask God to show you, with growing clarity, your function in the church.

> Staying faithful to God first is the best and only trustworthy foundation for true community.

Note that there are suggested group activities included in this session's "Between Sessions" material. Before dismissing today, you may want to find a date on everyone's calendars when most, if not all, of the group could gather for about an hour.

BETWEEN SESSIONS

PERSONAL REFLECTION

Take time in personal reflection to think about the following questions. If you would like, use the journaling space at the end of this session to record your thoughts.

- How deep are your roots in the local church? Do you need to settle in and connect more closely with the family of God in your church?
- What are signs in your life that you are beginning to wander and pull up roots from your local church? What can you do to make sure you stay planted where God has put you?
- What is your position in God's family? What are your unique functions?
- What can you do to reach out to any individuals you know who used to be active in your church, let them know they are missed, and invite them back? (More about this in the "Group Actions" section below.)
- How can you encourage and inspire others to find their function in the church, set down deep roots, and experience greater spiritual growth?

GROUP ACTIONS

Find an hour or so between regular meetings to get together as many of your small group members as possible to work through the following "body-building" activities.

WELCOME BACK

1. Using the first column of the chart, make a list of people you know who used to be an active part of your church but have pulled up roots and, as far as you're aware, are not part of a local church at this time.

Name	Who Will Contact This Person?	Report

2. Pray, as a group, for each of these people … by name.
3. Using the second column of the chart, talk about who in your group knows them best and is willing to call, text, email, or visit them.
4. In the coming week or two, contact everyone on the list and let them know they are missed, being prayed for, and invite them back. Let them know that your church will be stronger and a better place when they are connected again.
5. Be sure to report on the contact at a future meeting and use the third column of the chart to note pertinent information. Pray again for each of these people.

YOU MATTER AND YOU ARE LOVED

At the same get-together, briefly identify one person or family in your church who might be feeling forgotten or uncared for. Then pick one way you can reach out to them and let them know that they matter and are loved. It could be a letter from your group, a visit, a gift, or some other expression of love. The key is that you find a way to remind them of the spiritual reality that they are part of God's family and the local church. Let them know they matter.

> God will never strip us of our position or title in Christ.

PERSONAL ACTIONS
FUNCTIONING IN THE FAMILY

Make a list of one to three functions you have in your local church. Then, write down one step of growth you can take to further develop in this specific ministry. Pray and ask the Holy Spirit to empower and lead you to serve in this place of ministry with greater passion, effectiveness, and commitment. Finally, be sure to tell your small group members about this step of faith you have taken.

Function 1: _____

My next step of growth:

My prayer:

Function 2: _____

My next step of growth:

My prayer:

Function 3: _____

My next step of growth:

My prayer:

SPURS AND ENCOURAGEMENT

Hebrews 10:23–24 calls us to action. We are to "spur one another on toward love and good deeds." We are also to "encourage one another." Set a personal goal to "spur" or "encourage" a brother or sister in Christ this coming week. Use the space provided to set a plan to take action.

Who: _____

Will I "spur" on (challenge) or "encourage" (cheer)? And how will I do it?

When will I do it?

How did this go?

Keep a record and let your group know how this exercise went. Just a little warning: If you start spurring people on and encouraging them, they will probably start doing the same to you ... and this is a very good thing!

RECOMMENDED READING

As you reflect on what God is teaching you through this session, read or reread chapter 3 of *The God-First Life* by Stovall Weems. In preparation for the next session, read chapter 6.

JOURNAL, REFLECTIONS, AND NOTES

SPACE FOR THE SOUL TO BREATHE

Leave Your Problems Behind and Enter into God's Presence

The God-first life is saturated with worship. When we seek first God and his kingdom, we find ourselves looking forward to times we can gather with other Christians to sing, celebrate, pray, hear the Word preached, and enjoy the fellowship of brothers and sisters in Christ. But the God-first life also leads to worship that spills out of formal services and gatherings. Worship can happen as we drive in the car by ourselves, in the middle of a challenging business meeting, while caring for three little children at home, lying in bed at the end of a crazy day ... all of these become opportunities for worship when we live a God-first life. When a Christian is seeking first the things of God, worship services become sweet and rich with God's presence. And the ordinary experiences of life, even the tough moments, become opportunities to worship.

INTRODUCTION

They went on a mission trip. They just wanted to tell people about Jesus and help those in need. What could go wrong?

The answer is ... everything!

To start with, they bumped into a woman who was in deep distress and pain, and she started mocking them and interrupting their times of ministry. They kept trying to serve and do their mission work, but this broken and confused woman decided to follow them around and taunt them over and over again.

Things kept getting worse. Before they knew it, these two guys had their mission trip turned upside down when false accusations were made about them, and the people they were trying to reach became a mob that turned against them. Things were going downhill fast!

This mission trip was to a country where "criminals" could be beaten publicly, something these guys knew when they were sent out. If you go on a mission trip in some places, you do so understanding that you must accept dangers as part of the deal.

Before they knew it, they were both strapped up and beaten within an inch of their lives. To make matters worse, they were tossed in the local jail for the night.

What do you do when you have taken a risk to follow Jesus, tell others about him, share his love, and everything seems to go wrong? How do you respond after you have been lied about, ganged up on, beaten, and falsely thrown in jail? For these guys, the answer was ... worship!

In chains, their bodies still racked with mind-numbing pain, these two guys decided to continue their mission trip by holding a worship service in a jail cell in the middle of the night. They began to pray and sing praise songs.

What must the other prisoners have thought? As music filled the cellblock, as prayers filled the air, as bloodied and beaten lips lifted up words of worship ... the jail became a sanctuary! Can you imagine the third-shift jail guard hearing the songs of praise and passionate prayers echoing through the jail? How could these guys be singing after all they had suffered?

The mission trip began with street-witnessing and ended in jail. And, in this jail, through the power of worship, God showed up. A revival broke out. The late-shift guard gave his heart to Jesus! If you want to read the whole story, it is recorded in the sixteenth chapter of the book of Acts. Check it out sometime.

> Worship is how we create
> intimacy with God.

TALK ABOUT IT

When you hear the word *worship*, what ideas, images, and activities come to your mind?

or

How can a person facing great pain, hurt, and even injustice still dare to worship and praise God?

> The more we press into God, the more
> we pull away from our flesh.

VIDEO TEACHING NOTES

As you watch the video teaching segment for session 3, featuring Stovall Weems, use the following outline to record anything that stands out to you.

A lifestyle of worship and the act of worship

Worship engages the heart

2 Chronicles 5, a foreshadowing of New Testament worship

Worship is an "at that moment experience" with God

Through praise and worship, we unleash the power of God

Praise is the bridge of hope

Loving God with our heart, soul, mind, and strength

Worship God with your *strength*

Worship God with your *mind*

Worship God with your *soul*

Worship God with your *heart*

> The goal of worship is to engage,
> encounter, and experience the presence
> of the everlasting God.

VIDEO DISCUSSION AND BIBLE STUDY

1. Tell about a time when you were discouraged and worn out, but you began to worship anyway. Describe how God showed up for you.

   Why do you think worship is so powerful in these kinds of situations?

2. Stovall talks about how we can connect with God in many places and in many ways. We can worship while we drive down the road, as we lie in bed, in a church service, and in almost any place. Where is a place you really connect well with God and find yourself worshiping naturally? What is it about this place that draws you into the presence of God and helps you connect with him?

We can worship anytime and anywhere!

3. **Read:** 2 Chronicles 5:11–14. What happened as the people of God got together and drew near to God in worship?

What are some of the ways that the glory of the Lord shows up when his people worship him today?

4. Stovall talks about how worship is designed to be an "at that moment experience," where we can enter right into the very presence of God. How have you experienced this reality in your life as a worshiper?

> The Word of God engages the mind ...
> worship engages the heart.

5. If we lived each day with a deep personal realization that the presence and glory of God actually dwells in us, how might this help to subdue our flesh and direct our lifestyle choices?

6. **Read:** Psalm 8:1–2. In this psalm David declares that through praise, we achieve victory over our enemies. God unleashes power in worship! Tell about a time you experienced being strengthened and empowered through meeting God in worship.

How can consistent worship become a source of heavenly strength as you walk through each day?

7. What do you think Stovall means when he says we can "praise our way through hard times"?

What hard time are you facing right now, and what are a few practical ways you can praise your way through it? How can your group members pray for you, and praise with you, as you face this situation?

> Praise is the bridge from your present
> circumstances to a better day.

8. **Read:** Mark 12:28–31. How is this passage more about worship than it is about being perfect in our obedience?

If we worshiped God with all of our heart, soul, mind, and strength, how might this help us grow more obedient?

9. Work as a group to quickly list at least ten ways you can use your strength—actions you can take, decisions you can make, disciplines you can engage in—to worship God.

What is one item from the group list that you can begin doing this week, and how might loving God in this way help you grow as a worshiper?

10. What simple step of obedient faith and worship do you need to take in the coming week? How can your group members encourage you, pray for you, and cheer you on as you take this step?

> Putting God first, before my feelings,
> turns a simple move toward God
> into authentic worship.

CLOSING PRAYER

Take time as a group to pray in any of the following directions:

- Thank God for sending Jesus to make it possible for us to draw near to him in worship.
- Pray for wisdom to discover more ways to worship God in the flow of your day.
- Ask for God to help your heart be so committed to worship that when you gather with God's people, you will be fully engaged and give him the praise he deserves.
- Invite the Holy Spirit to whisper, nudge, or even shout to get your attention and draw you into worship as you walk through each day.
- Ask God to unleash his power in your life as you worship.
- Pray for your group members to invest their strength in worshiping God with greater frequency and intensity.

BETWEEN SESSIONS

PERSONAL REFLECTION

Take time in personal reflection to think about the following questions. If you would like, use the journaling space at the end of this session to record your thoughts.

- How has God lifted you up and encouraged you through worship?
- How can you make worship a more natural response when you face difficult times in your life?
- What one or two temptations are you facing right now, and how can you respond with worship each time these show up?
- What is one sorrow you are facing right now, and how can you worship with greater focus and passion as you walk through this?
- How can you worship God with more of your strength?

> Praise is the future picture of a better day.

PERSONAL ACTIONS
STRENGTH TO WORSHIP

Review the list your group made (see question 9 of the group study) and choose five ways you will engage your body in worship and use your strength to glorify God.

1.

2.

3.

4.

5.

Over the next couple of weeks, pay attention to how you are using your strength to praise God in both formal worship settings and the flow of an ordinary day. Be sure one or two of these physical expressions are new for you. If you have never lifted your hands in worship, give it a try. If you don't normally kneel when you pray, spend some time in the mornings and humbly kneel next to your bed.

FIND A PLACE AND GO THERE

Where do you experience God as you worship? Are there places that seem to naturally help you connect with God and praise him with greater passion? Maybe it is at a local park or lake. Perhaps it is in a certain chair in your home. It could be as you walk around your neighborhood or sit on your back porch. Identify a place (in or near your home) that really helps you worship and be sure to get there once a week for the next month.

List three or four reasons this space seems to draw you closer to God and helps you connect with Jesus:

-

-

-

-

CARING FOR GOD'S TEMPLE

The apostle Paul tells us that the Holy Spirit no longer dwells in man-made buildings, but in those who follow Jesus. Our bodies are actually the new temple of God.

Take a few minutes to ask God how you might better care for your body so that it will become a better place for him to dwell. It could be getting more sleep, exercising (or exercising more), watching what you eat, breaking a bad habit, or some other action. Write down one step you will take for the next thirty days:

I will care more for God's temple by:

At the end of thirty days, reflect on how this action has helped you grow as a worshiper.

> Worship is a momentary break from
> our own conflicted flesh and the
> challenges of this world.

RECOMMENDED READING

As you reflect on what God is teaching you through this session, read or reread chapter 6 of *The God-First Life* by Stovall Weems. In preparation for the next session, read chapter 4.

JOURNAL, REFLECTIONS, AND NOTES

DOING LIFE TOGETHER

Be Transformed through Community

When a person enters a new life with Jesus, they are adopted into a family. No Christian lives in isolation; we are part of a community of faith. One of God's greatest gifts, sources of strength, and conduits of wisdom is the church.

INTRODUCTION

Is it true that a turtle can die if it is left on its back?

The short and sad answer seems to be, "Yes."

If a turtle ends up on its back, and no one turns it over and puts it back on its feet, it can suffocate or starve. In this life-threatening moment, what an upside-down turtle needs is a helping hand. It needs someone who will flip it back onto its feet before it is too late. And, if there is no one to help, the turtle is in very serious trouble.

In the book of Ecclesiastes we read that we have something in common with that little turtle lying on its back. There are times when *we* need a helping hand!

> Two are better than one,
>   because they have a good return for their labor:
> If either of them falls down,
>   one can help the other up.
> But pity anyone who falls
>   and has no one to help them up.
>
> (Ecclesiastes 4:9–10)

This simple but clear picture is right in front of us. We need each other. We are better together. Community can save our life.

The Bible, from beginning to end, teaches that God designed us for relationship, for community, for connection. In the opening chapters of Genesis, we learn that man was not made to be alone. In the book of Revelation, we see all of God's people gathered in community, worshiping together.

We need each other. When we fall (and we all do), we need someone to help lift us up. We need a community of people who will love us, support us, encourage us, and challenge us. In his grace, God has given us such a community—it is called the church! When we are actively engaged in a local church, we are never alone. We have constant companionship and encouragement. We find friends and mentors and ministry. And, when we walk in fellowship with other Christians, if we happen to end up flat on our back like a little turtle, there is always someone near to flip us back onto our feet.

> Relationships are important to God and
> we were not created to live in isolation.

TALK ABOUT IT

Tell about a time you ended up flipped over on your back and God sent someone from his church to help get you back on your feet.

or

What are some of the gifts and benefits of being part of a vibrant local church?

> People don't fall into community;
> they pursue it.

VIDEO TEACHING NOTES

As you watch the video teaching segment for session 4, featuring Stovall Weems, use the following outline to record anything that stands out to you.

Connection versus community

The importance of relationships

Do the things you did at first (lessons from Ephesus)

The value of small groups

Fellowship (*koinonia* ... community)

Community ... communing ... communion

All the "one anothers"

Some blessings and miracles are received in community

Spiritual maturity is accelerated in small groups

VIDEO DISCUSSION AND BIBLE STUDY

1. How can social media create a false sense of being connected and having many "friends" but also cause a sense of isolation?

How is being connected different than being in community?

2. Respond to this statement: We were created for community and life is not right when we live in isolation.

> Deep community will not happen if we value busyness over relationships.

3. **Read:** Revelation 2:2–5 and Acts 19:8–10. What were some of the things that the believers in Ephesus did that helped put God first in their lives? What can we learn from their example?

4. In Acts 19 (verses 1–7) we read that Paul arrived in Ephesus to find twelve disciples who gathered regularly. Why is this kind of cluster of believers important to build community?

Tell about a small group experience (now or in the past) during which you grew spiritually and how community contributed to that growth.

5. **Read:** Acts 2:42–47. As you read this passage, note the ways that the followers of Jesus were living the God-first life in community with each other.

What might happen if believers today experienced this level of community and mutual care?

6. Stovall makes this statement: "There are many commands in the Bible that you can't obey unless you are planted in a local church ... in community." What are some of these commands?

7. The many "one another" passages in the Bible call us to a deep level of community. As volunteers take turns reading the following verses, write the various ways we support each other.

John 13:34

Romans 12:10

Romans 12:16

Romans 15:7

Galatians 5:13

Ephesians 4:32

Ephesians 5:21

Colossians 3:16

Hebrews 10:24

What are a few practical ways we can live out these "one another" exhortations in the flow of our community life together?

The God-first life is not meant to
be lived out on your own. In fact,
it really can't be done.

8. Describe a time that God built you up through community in *one* of these ways:

❑ Through a word of encouragement
❑ Through a firm challenge
❑ Through an act of service
❑ Through confession and the healing that followed

Who is someone you could build up in one of these areas, and what action will you take?

9. Stovall says that there are some blessings we will never get if we do not become part of a small group. Do you agree and if so, why? Do you disagree and if so, why?

What are some blessings we might never experience if we are not in a group?

10. How can a small group become a place for intimate sharing, honest confession, and high levels of spiritual growth?

Why is confidentiality absolutely essential in a small group? If confidentiality is broken, what can happen to the trust and spirit of a group?

> In the God-first life, when order is restored, blessing is released.

11. How can God use community to grow and mature you in ways that you might not grow otherwise?

CLOSING PRAYER

Take time as a group to pray in any of the following directions:

- Thank God that he has not designed us for isolation but for community.
- Pray for yourself, your group members, and your whole church to discover the gift and value of small groups.
- Confess where you have isolated yourself and pulled away from community.
- Ask God to help you live out the many "one another" commands of the Bible.
- Praise God for the good things he has done in your life through past small groups you have been part of (or the group you are presently in).
- Pray for the small group leaders in your church.

> When we are in community we are strengthened by one another.

BETWEEN SESSIONS

PERSONAL REFLECTION

Take time in personal reflection to think about the following questions. If you would like, use the journaling space at the end of this session to record your thoughts.

- Where are you on your back and in need of others to come and help you up?
- Who is one Christian friend on his or her back right now and in need of help? What will you do in response to their need?
- Are you just connected to people or really in community? How can you go deeper in relationships and move toward significant community?
- Are you contributing to your small group in significant ways through engagement, prayer, sharing, loving, attendance, and encouragement? What can you do to connect more deeply in your group?
- How do you isolate yourself, and how can you resist the temptation to pull away from others?
- What are some blessings you are receiving right now through community with other Christians?

> Give and sow whatever it is
> you want and desire.

PERSONAL ACTIONS
BLESSING IDENTIFICATION

In the journaling space or on a separate piece of paper, list twenty or more blessings that can come to your life if you decide to take the chance to live in authentic community with other Christians. Think long and hard. Do a Google search of "one another passages in the Bible" and discover many of the good things you can experience when you live in community with God's people.

Each day for the coming month, reflect on one of these potential blessings and pray that you will see this grow in your life as you seek to live in community.

THANKS FOR THE BLESSINGS

Through the years, and in recent days, God has blessed you through the community of other Christians. Write down the names of three people God has used to bless you. Then, identify two or three ways God has brought blessing into your life through that specific person. Finally, decide on one way you can express appreciation to this person ... and do it!

Person #1:
Ways I have been blessed through this person:

1.

2.

3.

How I can express my appreciation:

Person #2:
Ways I have been blessed through this person:

1.

2.

3.

How I can express my appreciation:

Person #3:
Ways I have been blessed through this person:

1.

2.

3.

How I can express my appreciation:

> Many times God speaks to
> us through other people.

TURTLE SUPPORT

Identify one staff member or church board member who is going through a hard time. Decide how you can come to their side and help get them back on their feet. What action, prayer, gift, support, or encouragement can you offer to flip this person over and thus extend the love of God's community?

Do the same with one person in your congregation who is not in leadership but who serves humbly and quietly without being noticed and is also going through a hard time.

RECOMMENDED READING

As you reflect on what God is teaching you through this session, read or reread chapter 4 of *The God-First Life* by Stovall Weems. In preparation for the next session, read chapters 5 and 8.

JOURNAL, REFLECTIONS, AND NOTES

_____

_____

_____

_____

_____

_____

_____

_____

_____

_____

_____

_____

_____

_____

_____

_____

_____

_____

_____

ARE YOU READY FOR GREATNESS?

Serve Others with Your Time and Resources

Being a Christian is not a spectator sport. Jesus did not die on the cross and rise again from the grave so we could all sit in church for an hour a week and then go home. He calls us to serve in his name. Jesus first modeled service and then he invited us into the adventure and joy of serving him, the church, and the world.

INTRODUCTION

Rosa came to faith in Jesus on a road paved with service.

A group of women in a local church served in a clothing closet ministry. Twice a week they opened their doors for people from their community to come and receive free clothing. They did not force Jesus on people, but they showed his love, talked about his care, and prayed for anyone who wanted to ask God for help.

Rosa showed up to get some clothing. She was in her fifties, had never needed help like this before, but she had come on hard times. The women at the clothing closet were so kind. They did not judge her. They cared. They even offered to pray for Rosa and her family, which she gladly accepted. They explained that people in the church gave clothes and money to provide for people like Rosa because they love Jesus and the people in their community.

Before she left, Rosa was so touched that she asked if she could come back again, not for more clothes, but to help give clothes to other women in need. Of course they said yes! Rosa began to serve before she was a Christian. Eventually, the women who worked with Rosa in the women's clothing closet invited her to church. She came, heard the gospel, and came forward to receive Jesus. She also kept serving in the clothing ministry and began to volunteer on the hospitality team as well.

About six months later, guess who was leading the women's clothing closet ministry? Guess who was having the time of her life? Guess who was praying for other women who had found themselves in hard times? Rosa came for clothes, but what she received was Jesus and a call to meaningful and life-changing service. God's love, grace, and forgiveness became hers. Now she leads the very ministry that first connected her to the local church.

> The local church is the vehicle that Jesus left on earth to be his hands and feet.

TALK ABOUT IT

Share a story about someone in your church who lives a life of exemplary service. How do you see Jesus alive in this person?

or

What is a ministry of service in your church that opens the door for people to come to faith in Jesus? How is God using this ministry to impact lives?

> Serving is not something we do;
> serving is who we are.

VIDEO TEACHING NOTES

As you watch the video teaching segment for session 5, featuring Stovall Weems, use the following outline to record anything that stands out to you.

A journey into service

Do all things to the best of your ability and for the Lord

Being faithful in little things as God opens doors for bigger things

Jesus came to serve and to give his life

Servants first, leaders second

The service of tithing

Giving the first 10 percent

Making one-time decisions

We are called to serve God with our time,
our talents, and our treasure.

VIDEO DISCUSSION AND BIBLE STUDY

1. Tell about a time you served in a ministry that demanded a humble spirit and willingness to do something that many people might avoid.

   How did this experience impact your life and grow your faith?

2. **Read:** Colossians 3:23–24. Describe a ministry experience in which you started doing something for *people* and grew discouraged, but finally realized you were actually serving *God*. How did your attitude and actions change when you realized you were working for the Lord?

   How did this simple act of service open the door for greater opportunities to serve Jesus?

   > Do you see yourself as a leader who serves or a servant who has opportunities to lead?

3. Why is it important for followers of Jesus to submit to godly authority and serve humbly, even when they think they might have more to offer? What could we miss if we decline such places of ministry?

4. **Read:** Matthew 20:25–28. What contrast does Jesus draw between leaders in the church and leaders in the world? What does Jesus say is the prerequisite to greatness in his kingdom, and what do you think he is trying to teach us?

5. In Matthew 20:28, Jesus articulates his life mission statement. What was Jesus' life all about? What are some examples, from the Gospels, of how Jesus lived out his mission statement?

6. **Read:** Philippians 2:5–11. What do you learn about the humility and servant-heart of Jesus in this passage? If you are going to be more like Jesus, what actions need to change in your life?

> Jesus, the Son of God, identified
> himself first of all as a servant.

7. **Read:** John 13:2–5, 12–17. What does this passage teach you about the character and heart of Jesus? What does Jesus call his followers to do?

In our day and age, what does it look like to wash other people's feet?

8. Consider an area of service in your church or community that really fits with your gifting and passions. Briefly discuss with your fellow group members what you could do to engage more fully in that area of service.

9. Why is giving the first 10 percent of your income to God's work a sign of a God-first life? If you have tried giving God the first of your financial resources, what happened in your heart and life?

Tithing is the sacred portion of your income … it is holy to the Lord.

10. What is a next step God wants you to take in serving with your time, talents, or tithe? How can your small group members pray for you and encourage you in this step of faithful service?

CLOSING PRAYER

Take time as a group to pray in any of the following directions:

- Thank God for the opportunities he has provided for you to serve others.
- Ask God to help you always do your best and to serve as if it is all for him ... because it is.
- Pray for humility to serve well in the little things that few people will notice.
- Thank Jesus for the many ways he has served you, including dying on the cross.
- Surrender your resources to God and commit to live with open hands, giving the first 10 percent to him and keeping the rest available to him.

> The God-first life means laying down the privileges we have come to expect and being willing to see ourselves as servants first.

BETWEEN SESSIONS

PERSONAL REFLECTION

Take time in personal reflection to think about the following questions.
If you would like, use the journaling space at the end of this session to
record your thoughts.

- Are there certain kinds of service and ministry that you avoid?
  Why do you avoid them, and is there something that needs to
  change in your attitude?
- Where is one place you need to serve with greater passion and
  commitment and become more aware that your service is not for
  people but for God?
- What examples of service did Jesus offer when he walked on this
  earth, and how can you follow his example in your daily life?
- Are you giving God 10 percent? Are you giving your first 10
  percent? What step can you take toward greater faithfulness in
  your personal stewardship?

PERSONAL ACTIONS
BEING FAITHFUL IN LITTLE

We live in a day and age where people like getting credit. We are not
quick to serve in obscurity. But God is clear that we need to be faithful
in little things so he can call us to great things.

Identify one area of service you can engage in that will be done
with little or no recognition. Make a decision to do this for the glory
of Jesus, even if no one else ever sees you do it. Keep a journal of what
Jesus does in you and through you. This can be done in your home, at
your workplace, your school, in your neighborhood, your church, or
anywhere you go.

My simple act of service: _____

Week 1 . . . what I learned:
What did God teach me about myself?

How did God work in me and grow me?

How did God work through me to bless and impact others?

Week 2 . . . what I learned:
What did God teach me about myself?

How did God work in me and grow me?

How did God work through me to bless and impact others?

Week 3 ... what I learned:
What did God teach me about myself?

How did God work in me and grow me?

How did God work through me to bless and impact others?

Final lessons ... what did I learn about God?

> There are certain things about knowing Jesus that you will never understand until you serve.

NOTICING FAITHFUL SERVICE

In the next week, take time to look around your church and identify three to five people who are serving faithfully in a place where most people do not notice. (Perhaps you might walk around on a Sunday or some other time when programs are happening.) Use the space provided to gather your information: name, place of ministry, and one or two ways you see God using this person to serve in the name of Jesus and bless others. Then, write a note to each of these people and thank them for serving. Let them know they are appreciated and how you see God working in them and through them.

Name: _____

Their ministry area: _____

One or two ways I see God at work through this person:

Name: _____

Their ministry area: _____

One or two ways I see God at work through this person:

Name: _____

Their ministry area: _____

One or two ways I see God at work through this person:

> Reaching out to others is really
> the love of God in action.

TITHING EXPERIMENT

Dare to try a thirty-day experiment where you give the first 10 percent of all you earn to the work of Jesus. Test God and see if he shows up, provides, and brings blessing to your life.

Keep a list of some of the blessings you experience in the thirty days that you do the tithe-test.

Blessings:

-

-

-

-

-

-

-

-

-

-

RECOMMENDED READING

As you reflect on what God is teaching you through this session, read or reread chapters 5 and 8 of *The God-First Life* by Stovall Weems. In preparation for the final session, read chapters 7, 9, and 10.

JOURNAL, REFLECTIONS, AND NOTES

FREE LIFE

Gain Real Freedom from the Past, in the Present, for the Future

True and lasting freedom begins when our minds are surrendered to God, he guides our thoughts, and the truth of the Bible directs our daily decisions. Satan is working overtime to lie, deceive, and mislead you. God's Word and truth are the perfect antidote to overcome the deception of the enemy and set you free!

INTRODUCTION

When you look closely, you will discover that the message of the world and the teaching of the Bible are radically different. The dilemma is that most of us spend so much time intersecting with the world that we adopt wrong thinking and misguided attitudes—and hardly notice it happening. This is why God wants us to read the Bible daily and let his truth sink deep into our souls. We need a compass to keep us on track when the world is feeding us lies that can send us in the wrong direction and shipwreck our lives.

If we listen to the voice of the world, we will believe that seeking our own desires and living with self-centered interests is just fine. But if we follow the teaching of the Bible, we will seek to serve as Jesus served, sacrifice for others, and be humble enough to put others ahead of us.

If we buy the party line of the media and culture, we will accept, embrace, and even celebrate any and every form of sexual activity. But the Bible teaches us that there are clear boundaries for sexual expression and holiness. We can't just do whatever we want, with whomever we want, whenever we want! Sexual intimacy is designed and reserved for a man and a woman in the covenant relationship of marriage.

Those who adopt the thinking of the world believe that when someone hurts them, they have the right to retaliate, take revenge, or at least harbor anger and resentment. Biblical Christians know that when they are wronged they are called to extend forgiveness, even when it is very difficult.

Yes, the world, media, and culture send consistent and powerful messages designed to shape our thinking and behavior. So God gives us his Word to clear our minds and send us in a loving, truth-filled direction that is often diametrically opposed to those messages. Anyone who wants to live a God-first life will make a decision to study the Bible and let God direct their steps. Sometimes following God's ways means living like a salmon that swims upstream against the current. It takes hard work and can be exhausting, but it is always a glorious adventure.

God's plan for you is a plan of freedom.

TALK ABOUT IT

Tell about a time you followed your instincts, gut, or sense of what seemed right and ended up going in the wrong direction or spiraling downward. What was the result of this wrong decision; what consequences did you face?

or

Talk about one area of your life where you feel like you are really working to swim against the cultural current and live God's way. How is the truth of the Bible giving you direction and strength to stay on the right track?

VIDEO TEACHING NOTES

As you watch the video teaching segment for session 6, featuring Stovall Weems, use the following outline to record anything that stands out to you.

Making sacred space to meet with God

Believing what the Bible says above what we think

Wrong thinking and errant beliefs lead to captivity

The lies, deceit, and bondage of the devil

The freedom, deliverance, and healing of Jesus

Jesus' first two miracles

Jesus wants to clean house and drive sin and brokenness out of your life

God loves you and he is on your side.

VIDEO DISCUSSION AND BIBLE STUDY

1. Where is a place you like to meet with your heavenly Father, spending time reading his Word and talking with him?

Why is it helpful and valuable to have a sacred place to meet with God?

2. What are some of the things that God's Word tells us about ourselves? Why is it important that we believe and receive what the Bible says about us and not accept what the world says?

3. Tell about a time that the truth of the Bible set you in a direction that was counter to what the world says is right. How did the Bible serve to protect you and keep you safe?

4. Name some of the wrong ideas and beliefs of our culture that lead people into bondage, brokenness, and addictions, or keep them from God's best for their lives.

> Wrong thinking and wrong believing is
> the starting point of all captivity.

5. **Read:** 2 Corinthians 10:3–6. What does it mean to take captive every thought and submit it to Jesus? What are some ways we can do this?

6. Give examples of behaviors, attitudes, or practices that can cause our thoughts to run wild and far away from God's truth. What can we do to avoid or cut off these behaviors?

7. **Read:** Romans 12:2. What role does the Bible have in the process of renewing our minds? How does knowledge of God's truth revealed in the Bible help us test our thoughts and attitudes and make sure they are honoring to him?

> Freedom in the God-first life is all about your new inner freedom working its way out into the rest of your life.

8. What are some ways we can get the truth of the Bible deep into our minds, saturating our thoughts and lives?

What is one step you can take in the coming days to get the truth of Scripture into your heart and mind with greater intentionality and frequency?

9. **Read:** Genesis 3:1–7. What were some of the tactics Satan used and what lies did he tell as he tried to lure human beings away from following God's will?

Make a list and be very specific:

-

-

-

-

-

How do you see Satan using these same tactics today?

10. How can we identify the tactics Satan is using against us personally and fight against them? Which of these tactics does Satan use most often against you, and how can your group members pray for you and support you as you resist the enemy's efforts to lie to and deceive you?

> When we focus less on ourselves and simply allow the Bible to speak for itself, we position ourselves to experience God's revelation and lasting change in our lives.

CLOSING PRAYER

Take time as a group to pray in any of the following directions:

- Thank God for giving us the Bible and for speaking clearly to his children.
- Ask God to help you read the Bible faithfully and to learn his truth as you do so.
- Invite the Holy Spirit to show you where your thinking and attitudes don't line up with God's truth revealed in the Bible.
- Dare to ask Jesus to drive out any sinful patterns from your life, even if it is painful and difficult.

> Getting to know God better is how you know how to change your life so you can start living according to his ways.

IN THE COMING DAYS

PERSONAL REFLECTION

Take time in personal reflection to think about the following questions.
If you would like, use the journaling space at the end of this session to
record your thoughts.

- If you have a place you meet regularly with God, how can you
  make this space more conducive to spiritual growth and connection with him?
- Are there sources of wrong thinking and worldly attitudes that
  you are letting flow into your heart and mind? If so, what can
  you do to cut these off?
- What are some ways that the truth of God, revealed in his
  Word, has set you free and pointed you in new directions of
  health and joy?
- If Jesus were to come to you with a custom-made whip, what
  would he want to drive out of the temple of your life so that you
  can live in greater freedom and joy?

> When we look at the Scriptures, we find a
> reflection of what we look like in Christ.

PERSONAL ACTIONS
EXPLORE SACRED SPACE

In the next week, do a little experiment. Try meeting with God in three
or four different spaces. Plan in advance and be intentional. Think of
places where you can get some uninterrupted time. Or, maybe choose
a place where you see people and encounter the needs around you. Be
creative and try some new options for your devotional time with God.
Journal what you learn. You might just discover some new options for
sacred space!

Space #1: _____
How I experienced God in this place ...

What I could do to make this place more conducive to connecting with God ...

Space #2: _____
How I experienced God in this place ...

What I could do to make this place more conducive to connecting with God ...

Space #3: _____
How I experienced God in this place ...

What I could do to make this place more conducive to connecting with God ...

A STRANGE REMINDER

If you enjoy crafts, you might enjoy this. Take some time and make your own "decorative whip." It could be from leather, vines, or whatever you want to use. Then, put this whip somewhere you will see it on a regular basis. Every time you see it, remember this session and ask Jesus to love you enough to drive the junk out of your life that does not honor him. If someone asks you about your "decorative whip," take the opportunity to explain what it symbolizes.

Jesus is passionate about your freedom.

CULTURE STUDY

God's Word is very clear about many things that our culture disagrees with. In the coming few days, pay attention to messages you see and hear. Take note of how the world's messages are dramatically different than what God says is right and best for us. Take the simple truths below and study how the world is propagating messages that are counter to what God says.

Use the following table to collect your thoughts:

God Says . . .	The Messages of the World on This Topic
Love your enemy and pray for people who treat you badly.	
Forgive those who have wronged you. Seek to forgive the way Jesus forgave you.	
Seek first God's kingdom and ways and he will take care of the rest.	
Don't gossip or speak poorly of other people.	
Be content with what you have and share freely with those in need.	
Love God and love your neighbor; these are the most important things you could ever do.	

Come up with a couple of categories of your own ...

God Says ...	The Messages of the World on This Topic

> By seeking God's kingdom and righteousness first, we can know and experience freedom in every part of our lives.

RECOMMENDED READING

As you reflect on what God is teaching you through this session, read or reread chapters 7, 9, and 10 of *The God-First Life* by Stovall Weems.

JOURNAL, REFLECTIONS, AND NOTES

SMALL GROUP LEADER HELPS

To ensure a successful small group experience, read the following information before beginning.

GROUP PREPARATION

Whether your small group has been meeting together for years or is gathering for the first time, be sure to designate a consistent time and place to work through the six sessions. Once you establish the when and where of your times together, select a facilitator who will keep discussions on track and an eye on the clock. If you choose to rotate this responsibility, assign the six sessions to their respective facilitators up front, so that group members can prepare their thoughts and questions prior to the session they are responsible for leading. Follow the same assignment procedure should your group want to serve any snacks/beverages.

A NOTE TO FACILITATORS

As facilitator, you are responsible for honoring the agreed-upon timeframe of each meeting, for prompting helpful discussion among your group, and for keeping the dialogue equitable by drawing out quieter members and helping more talkative members to remember that others' insights are valued in your group.

You might find it helpful to preview each session's video teaching segment and then scan the discussion questions and Bible passages that pertain to it, highlighting various questions that you want to be sure to cover during your group's meeting. Ask God in advance of your time together to guide your group's discussion, and then be sensitive to the direction he wishes to lead.

Urge group members to bring their study guide, pen, and a Bible to every gathering. Encourage them to consider buying a copy of *The God-First Life* book by Stovall Weems to supplement this study.

SESSION FORMAT

Each session of the study guide includes the following group components:

- **"Introduction"** — an entrée to the session's topic, which may be read by a volunteer or summarized by the facilitator
- **"Talk About It"** — icebreaker questions that relate to the session topic and invite input from every group member (select one, or use both options if time permits)
- **"Video Teaching Notes"** — an outline of the session's 12–16 minute video teaching for group members to follow along and take notes if they wish
- **"Video Discussion and Bible Study"** — video-related and Bible exploration questions that reinforce the session content and elicit personal input from every group member
- **"Closing Prayer"** — several prayer cues to guide group members in closing prayer

Additionally, in each session you will find a **"Between Sessions"** section that includes suggestions for personal response, a journaling opportunity, and recommended reading from *The God-First Life* book.

One of the "Between Sessions" sections — for session 2 — also features suggested group activities. A reminder is included at the end of the group study for this session so that members might schedule this extra gathering before departing for the day.

THE GOD FIRST LIFE NETWORK

 GODFIRSTLIFENETWORK.COM

PASTORS & LEADERS VISIT

GODFIRSTLIFENETWORK.COM FOR

FREE RESOURCES

FREE CHURCH GROWTH RESOURCES

FREE ASSIMILATION RESOURCES

FREE GROUP LEADER RESOURCES

The God-First Life

Uncomplicate Your Life,
God's Way

Stovall Weems

**A simple and sustainable path to a
deep and satisfying walk with Christ**

There are thousands of how-to books for improving various areas of life—self, relationships, finances, fitness, business, marriage, family. And there are nearly as many books written for believers offering a framework for the "right" approach to a new life in God.

What if it were possible, Pastor Stovall Weems asks, to boil it all down to one practical, uncomplicated principle that would yield the vibrant, purposeful spiritual life so many are looking for? What if, in our relationship with God, we had one simple and sustainable touch point to experience a deep and satisfying walk with Christ?

In *The God-First Life*, Weems shows that true success in our walk with God and in life in general is not an issue of need, but an issue of order. Brilliantly unpacking the simple Scripture in Matthew 6:33, he gives a fresh and practical perspective on what Christian "discipleship" is all about, and brings clarity, depth, and simplicity to core truths that have been misunderstood by many Christians and non-Christians alike.